ADOPTION

by Karen Bryant-Mole

Consultant: John Hall,
Counselling Support Manager of ChildLine

Wayland

Adoption

Bullying

Child Abuse

Death

Growing Up

Splitting Up

Step Families

Designed by Helen White
Edited by Deb Elliott

We gratefully acknowledge the assistance of the following people in the production of this book:
Dr Rachel Waugh, Principal Clinical Psychologist,
Great Ormond Street Hospital

All the words in **bold** are explained in the glossary on page 31.

This edition published in 1994 by Wayland (Publishers) Ltd

First published in 1992 by Wayland (Publishers) Limited
61 Western Road, Hove, East Sussex BN3 1JD

British Library Cataloguing in Publication Data
Bryant – Mole, Karen
Adoption. – (What's Happening? Series)
I. Title II. Series
362.7

HARDBACK ISBN 0-7502-0444-3

PAPERBACK ISBN 0-7502-1377-9

Phototypeset by White Design
Printed and bound in Italy by G. Canale & C. S. p. A.

CONTENTS

ELLIE AND MICHAEL

Ellie is nine years old. She likes singing, writing stories and listening to music. She hates Brussels sprouts and wearing scratchy jumpers. Ellie has a best friend called Anna and wants to be an actress when she grows up.

Michael is seven. He likes telling jokes and playing football. He hates tidying his bedroom and going shopping. He is not sure whether he will be a pilot or a milkman when he grows up.

Ellie and Michael sound like very ordinary children, don't they? But there is something special about them. It isn't something you can see just by looking at them. Nor is it something you can find out just by asking them what they like and don't like. What makes Ellie and Michael special is that they are both adopted. Being adopted means that the families Ellie and Michael live with now aren't the families that they were born into.

Ellie and Michael are special but they are not unusual. In fact, millions of people in the world are adopted. Not all of them are children, although of course they were nearly all young when they were first adopted. Now many of them are adults. There are shopkeepers, doctors, teachers, uncles, grannies and even great grannies who were adopted when they were younger.

RIGHT Being adopted isn't something you can see. All these children could be adopted, or perhaps none of them are.

WHY ARE CHILDREN ADOPTED?

Gemma knows that her mum and dad wanted her very much and that they were really happy when they found out she was coming to live with them. She loves to hear the story that her mum and dad tell her about the day she came home with them. Her favourite part is the bit when her dad tried to change her nappy for the first time and put it on back to front!

BELOW *This girl was adopted when she was one year old.*

Gemma used to wonder why her **birth parents** couldn't keep her. One day she asked her mum about it. Her mum told her that her birth parents were both very young when Gemma was born and they knew they wouldn't be able to look after her properly. They thought about what would be best for Gemma and decided that she would probably be happier with another family.

There are lots of different reasons why children are adopted. Perhaps the birth parents don't have enough money to bring up a child. Perhaps the birth mum or dad

are alone and can't manage to look after a child. Or perhaps, very sadly, the birth mum and dad die.

Sometimes, like Gemma's parents, the adoptive parents know why the birth parents couldn't keep the child, but sometimes even they don't know. The one thing all adopted children know is that the parents they have now wanted them very, very much.

ABOVE *Children are adopted for lots of different reasons.*

HOW DO CHILDREN GET NEW FAMILIES?

ABOVE Keith and Sue met a social worker, who decided whether they would be good parents or not.

Keith and Sue wanted to adopt a child. First of all they wrote to an **adoption agency**. Adoption agencies are special places that help to bring children and parents together. The **social workers** who work for adoption agencies take great care to try to find parents who will make good mums and dads.

Keith and Sue met a social worker who talked to them to find out what sort of parents they were likely to be. They were asked lots of questions. After that they had to wait to find out if the social worker thought they would be good parents. They were very nervous! When Keith and Sue heard that the adoption agency thought that they would make good parents they were delighted. One day the social worker told them about a boy called David. She said that Keith, Sue and David sounded just right for each other. When they met they knew she was right. After getting to know Keith and Sue, David moved in with them. David also met a **judge** in a court. The judge checked that everything was all right and said that the adoption could go ahead.

ABOVE *After a while David moved in with Keith and Sue.*

Not all children meet their new families in exactly this way. However, all adoptive parents have to be seen by adoption agencies to make sure that they will make good mums and dads. So, if you are adopted, it is not just you who are special, your mum and dad are pretty special too!

TELLING OTHER PEOPLE

ABOVE Sammy wasn't sure at first whether to tell people about being adopted.

Sammy is eight. He is adopted and loves watching American football and baseball.

Sometimes children who are adopted wonder whether or not they should tell other people about it. Usually it's best to do whatever you feel comfortable with. Sammy doesn't tell everyone he meets that he loves watching American football. In the same way he doesn't tell everyone he meets that he is adopted. You will probably find that there are times and places when it feels right to talk about being adopted.

Sammy's class were doing a project about the colour of people's eyes. They had to check whether they had eyes the same colour as their mother's or father's. Sammy told everyone that he didn't know the colour of his birth parents' eyes because he was adopted. The rest of the class were really interested. In fact they were so interested that they started a new project about families. They looked at lots of different sorts of families; families with adopted children, families where the mum and dad are **divorced** or have split up, families with only one child, families with foster children and one parent families.

Sammy chose to tell the class about being adopted. Everyone, whether they are adopted or not, can choose what they tell other people about themselves.

BELOW *In the end, Sammy told everyone in his class about being adopted.*

MY DAD'S A KING!

Some adopted children know a lot about their birth parents but many know very little. Often those children think about what their birth parents might look like or what jobs they might do.Craig used to wonder what his birth parents were like. He liked to think that they might be a king and queen. Craig began telling his friends that he was a prince. At first his friends were very impressed. Then Craig began acting like a prince too and showing off. His friends soon got fed up with this. One day his friend Matthew said, 'Liar! I don't think you're a prince at all.'

BELOW Craig liked making up stories about his birth parents.

ABOVE Sometimes children who aren't adopted pretend they are!

Craig knew it was just a story but he had told it to his friends as if it was the truth. The real truth was that Craig didn't know what sort of jobs his birth parents had. They could be anything. Perhaps things would have been different if he had told his friends that he *might* be a prince. Then they could all have joined in the make-believe. If you don't know very much about your birth parents you have probably wondered what kind of people they are. It can be good fun to make up stories about them. Children who aren't adopted sometimes make up stories about their parents too. One of the stories that they sometimes make up is that they are adopted! That's because everyone likes to feel special and they see being adopted as something special.

DESPERATE DAN

JOE

Children are adopted at lots of different ages and for all sorts of reasons. They have their own feelings about being adopted. This is how Joe feels:

'I'm eight now but I came to live with my mum and dad when I was three months old. I was too little to remember anything about my birth parents. I have freckles though and I often wonder whether either of them had freckles too. I love music and I play the piano. I do know that my birth dad was a musician, so perhaps I take after him.

'Apart from that I don't often think about being adopted. We live in a small village where we have lots of friends. My mum told just about everyone she knew that they were hoping to adopt me. If she hadn't they would have thought it was very strange for her to have no children one day and a three-month-old baby the next! My friends all know that I am adopted but it isn't something that we talk about particularly.

'Once when we were on holiday I made friends with this boy. I told him I was adopted and he kept going on about it. He wanted to know what it felt like! He seemed to think it must be strange. I said it didn't feel like anything in particular. I can't think of anything else to say about being adopted really.'

OPPOSITE *Being adopted isn't something Joe thinks about very often. He lives in a small village where everyone knows he is adopted. Everyone takes it for granted.*

KATE

Not all children are adopted when they are babies. Kate was older:

'When I was three and my brother was five, my mum had twins. Then my dad left and she had to look after all four of us by herself. She used to get cross a lot. There was a social worker who came to visit us and we all decided that my mum needed a rest so my brother and I went to stay with **foster parents**. Foster parents are people who look after you for a while. You still belong to your mum and dad, but stay with them.

'The social worker hoped that we would be able to go back and live with my mum and so did I but it just didn't work out. In the end everyone felt that it would probably be better for me and my brother if we were adopted. I didn't really like the idea. My foster parents helped me make a Life Story Book. I liked that. It told the story of my life until then. I helped to stick in photos.

ABOVE Kate is making a Life Story Book about her life until now.

'My mum wanted my brother and me to stay together and it took quite a long time to find a new family who wanted two children. Then we met Dave and Jill. I have shown them my Life Story Book so they know what happened to me before I came to live with them.

'When we first moved in my brother was really naughty. He used to break things on purpose and once he even said he would run away! I think he wanted to see whether they really loved us. I called them Jill and Dave for a long time but now I call them mum and dad. We call my other mum my birth mum. Sometimes I still miss her and get upset and cry about it but I have a photo of her in my Life Story Book that I like looking at.'

BELOW *After some time Kate and her brother met Jill and Dave, their new parents.*

MARTIN

RIGHT Martin found out by accident that he was adopted, and at first he was very upset.

Most children, whether they are adopted as babies or when they are older, grow up knowing they are adopted. A few children, like Martin, do not find out until later.

'All along I felt there was something not quite right. I didn't look at all like my mum or dad. When I mentioned it to mum she used to say things like "Oh, but you look just like my father when he was a boy." I had seen photos of grandpa as a boy but I didn't think I looked like him at all. One day I asked mum how old I was when I first started to walk. She got a funny look on her face and said she wasn't sure because it was so long ago. But I thought she ought to remember.

'Last year when we were getting ready to go on holiday my dad asked me to get the **passports** out of his desk. While I was looking for them I found some papers that said that I'd been adopted when I was two. It was a real shock. I couldn't believe it. Then I remembered all the little things that had felt not quite right and it suddenly all made sense. I was really upset though. Why hadn't mum and dad told me? They said they thought it would be best for me not to know but I think it would have been better if I had known.

'After that we used to talk about me being adopted but it was a long time before I stopped feeling angry. I do feel much happier now, knowing that I am adopted. Everything seems to have fallen into place and I don't feel all wrong any more.'

ABOVE *Once Martin and his parents had talked about everything he felt much happier.*

ARE ADOPTED CHILDREN DIFFERENT?

Sometimes children who are adopted wonder if that makes them somehow different from other children.

ABOVE Joe

Joe, Kate and Martin were asked whether they felt different to other children.

Joe: 'I don't feel any different at all to my friends. I know I am adopted. It's part of my life but it doesn't make me any different.'

Kate: 'Sometimes I feel different because I have had a birth family, a foster family and an adoptive family and none of my friends have. But I'm not different apart from that.'

Martin: 'I did feel very different before I knew I was adopted. I can't exactly say how, it was just that something didn't feel right. Once I knew I was adopted I still felt a bit different but not peculiar or weird. It was more that finding out you are adopted isn't something that happens to many children.'

Different is a strange word. If you think about it, everyone, whether they are adopted or not, is different. No two people are exactly alike, even twins. Everyone has their own likes and dislikes and ways of behaving. Lots of things go into making the person you are and one of them might be that you are adopted.

There is a word that means 'not the same as anything or anyone else'. That word is 'unique' and each of us, adopted or not, is unique.

ABOVE *Kate*

LEFT *Martin*

WHY ARE THEY CROSS WITH ME?

Lloyd always seemed to be in trouble with his mum and dad. He'd been told off for leaving his bike in the garden. He had been banned from watching television for a week because he had broken the video and now his mum was yelling at him because he'd gone to play with John after school. Suddenly Lloyd shouted out,

BELOW Lloyd was often in trouble.

ABOVE Lloyd's mum told him he was her real son.

'You're yelling at me because I'm adopted. If I was your real son you wouldn't be cross with me, would you?'

His mum was stunned. She told him he was her real son and that shouting at him had nothing to do with being adopted. He wasn't sure. Why was she so cross? And what about all the other times? Lloyd's mum could see that he had been worrying about it so they thought about it together. Why did he get into trouble for leaving his bike out? Because it was raining and the bike would get rusty. Why was he banned from watching television? Because he had promised never to touch the video and broken his promise. Why was she yelling at him now? Because he hadn't told her he was going to John's and she was worried about where he could be. Were any of those reasons to do with Lloyd being adopted?

HAVE I GOT TO BE GOOD?

ABOVE Dawn tried to be a perfect child to please her parents.

Dawn was adopted when she was ten. When she was adopted she was so pleased that she decided to be extra good. She didn't play in the garden, in case she got her clothes all messy. She didn't play noisy games and if her mum or dad asked her to do something she would do it immediately, in case they thought she didn't love them enough.

Dawn's mum and dad started to worry about her. She wasn't just good, she was too good. Dawn's mum asked her why she wouldn't play in the garden. At first Dawn said it was because she didn't want to. Then she managed to tell her mum about being scared in case they wouldn't like her if she got messy. She said she wanted to be good as a thank you to her mum and dad for adopting her. She also said she thought that if she wasn't good enough for them they might send her away.

Dawn's mum hugged her and told her that they didn't need thank yous. They didn't need her to be extra good or extra clever or extra anything. They just wanted her to be Dawn. She told Dawn that adopted children can't just be sent back and that she would never ever want to do that anyway.

All children, whether they are adopted or not, are sometimes good and sometimes naughty, good at some things and not so good at others. You don't have to try to be something you are not. Just be YOU!

ABOVE Dawn's mum told her that they just wanted her to be herself.

BROTHER AND SISTER!

ABOVE
Children often have to work quite hard at getting on together.

Harry and Lara are brother and sister. They are both adopted but not from the same birth family.

Harry likes making models and Lara likes kicking them over. They always want to watch different channels on the television and when they argue they each say it's the other's fault. Some days it makes their parents really cross.

Harry was sure that the reason he and his sister didn't get on was because they were adopted. One day he said to his parents, 'I bet you wish you'd never adopted us, don't you?' Their mum told them about something that had happened at her friend Sue's house. Sue had two children about the same age as Harry and Lara. While she and Sue were having a cup of coffee they heard a

terrible row coming from the next room.'Oh no, not another fight' said Sue. Harry's mum had to smile because they sounded just like Lara and Harry.

'Sue's children aren't adopted are they?' mum said to Lara and Harry, after telling them the story. She told them that sometimes children in families get on very well together and sometimes they don't but that it didn't really have anything to do with whether or not they are adopted.

ABOVE Lara and Harry's mum knows from her friends that all children argue, not just adopted children.

PART OF A FAMILY

Being an adopted child means being part of a family. One of the best things about being adopted is knowing that you are part of a family that really wanted you. That doesn't mean that everyone in your family has to be happy all the time or that things won't go wrong. That only happens in fairytale families.

BELOW AND RIGHT All adopted children are part of a family.

People in real families sometimes argue, they sometimes get cross and they sometimes do things which annoy each other. But people in real families also have fun together, they listen and talk with each other, they care for each other and they make each other happy. This is what being part of a family means to all children. If you are adopted you also know something extra special about your family. You know that your mum and dad wanted you very, very much.

FOR PARENTS AND TEACHERS

Studies show that the majority of adoption placements turn out very well. Occasionally, though, the children and their new families have problems. These problems are not always connected with adoption and might just as easily occur in families with no adopted children.

A research study by the National Children's Bureau showed that, at the age of seven, adopted children were doing as well as, and often better than, other children in the community. Further studies confirm that adoption is a satisfying experience for most children and families and a good way of providing family life for children who cannot be brought up by their birth parents.

There are several organizations which offer support to adoptive parents, adopted people and birth parents. These include:

After Adoption
2nd Floor Lloyds House
22 Lloyd Street
Manchester M2 5WA
Tel. 061 839 4930

National Organization for Counselling Adoptees and their Parents (NORCAP)
3 New High Street
Heddington
Oxford OX3 5AJ
Tel. 0865 750554

Parent to Parent Information on Adoption Service
Lower Boddington
Daventry
Northants NN11 6YB
Tel 0327 60295

Post Adoption Centre
8 Torriano Mews
Torriano Street
London NW5 2RZ

GLOSSARY

Adoption agency The place where people have to go if they want to adopt a child. The agency tries to make sure that they will be good parents.
Birth parents The people who gave birth to you.
Divorced Sometimes people who are married decide that they don't want to be married to each other any more. They ask a judge in a court to make this legal and then they are divorced.
Foster parents If a child's parents are unable to look after him or her for some reason, the child may go and live with foster parents for a while.
Judge The person in a court who makes decisions about what people can and cannot do.
Passport A small book with your name and photograph in it, which you take to a foreign country so that you can show where you are from.
Social worker A person who tries to help people live together happily.

BOOKS TO READ

Andy's Big Question Carolyn Nystrom (Lion Books, 1987)
How it Feels to be Adopted Jill Krementz (Victor Gollancz, hardback 1984, paperback 1991)
So You're Adopted! James Stanford (A. C. Donald, 1986)
Why Was I Adopted? Carol Livingstone (Angus and Robertson, 1978)

INDEX

Picture Acknowledgements
Chapel Studios (Zul Mukhida) 6, 7, 14, 18, 19, 20, 21 (bottom), 22, 23, 24, 25; Eye Ubiquitous 28; Jeff Isaac Greenburg 10, 11, 12, 13, 16, 17, 21 (top), 27, 29; Wayland cover, 9, 26; Zefa 5, 8.
Some of the people who are featured in this book are models. We gratefully acknowledge the help and co-operation of all those individuals who have been involved in this project.